HOW TO DRAW
EVERYTHING

THIS BOOK BELONGS TO:

....

VERSY

GET YOUR GIFT !

RECEIVE A COLORING BOOK AS A GIFT, IN WHICH
THE CHARACTERS AND OBJECTS FROM THIS BOOK
FALL INTO REAL LIFE.

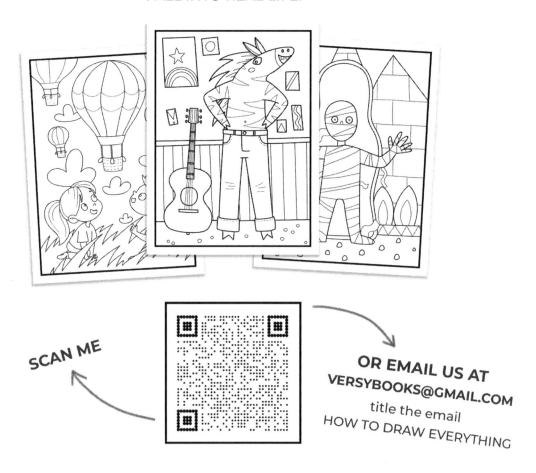

SCAN ME

OR EMAIL US AT
VERSYBOOKS@GMAIL.COM
title the email
HOW TO DRAW EVERYTHING

HOW TO DRAW EVERYTHING. for kids.

HOW TO USE THIS BOOK

TAKE PAPER AND YOUR FAVORITE DRAWING MATERIALS

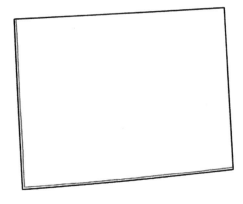

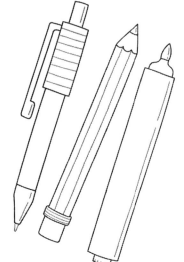

❚ FOLLOW STEP-BY-STEP. DRAW THE LINES.

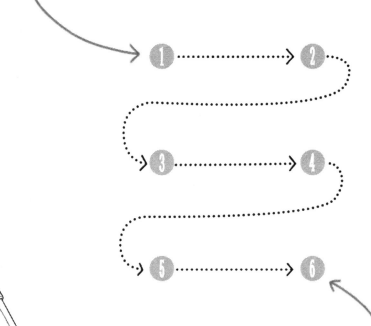

❚ ADD DETAILS TO THE DRAWING.

IF YOU DIDN'T GET DRAWING A PICTURE FIRST TIME, DON'T WORRY. TRACING FINAL PICTURE. THEN TRY TO DRAW IT YOURSELF AGAIN, FOLLOWING STEP-BY-STEP.

4

BANANA

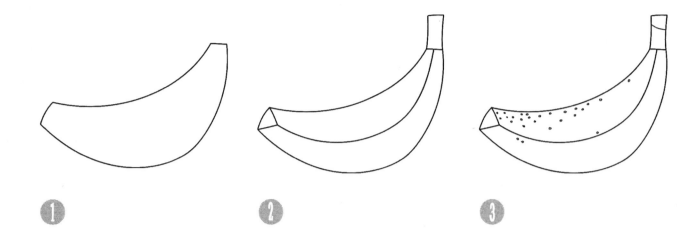

STRAWBERRY

6

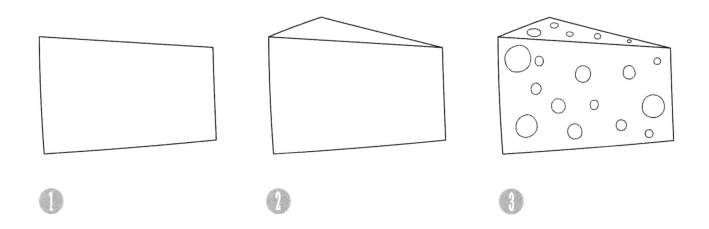

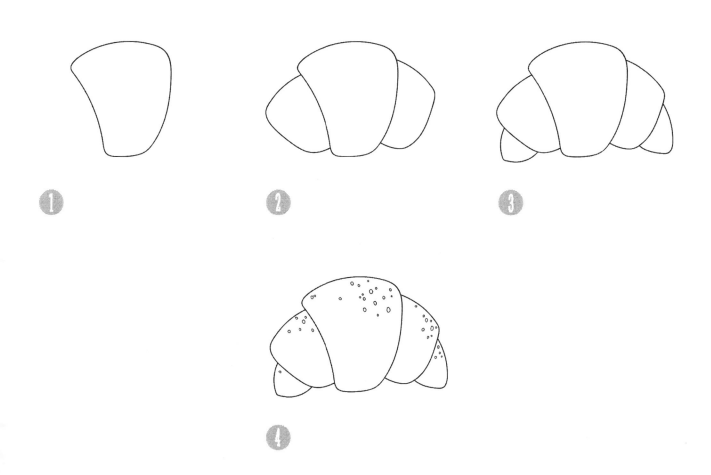

FORK

KNIFE

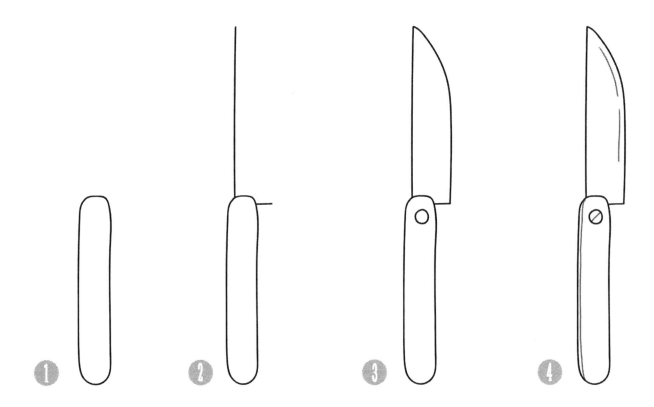

ESKIMO PIE

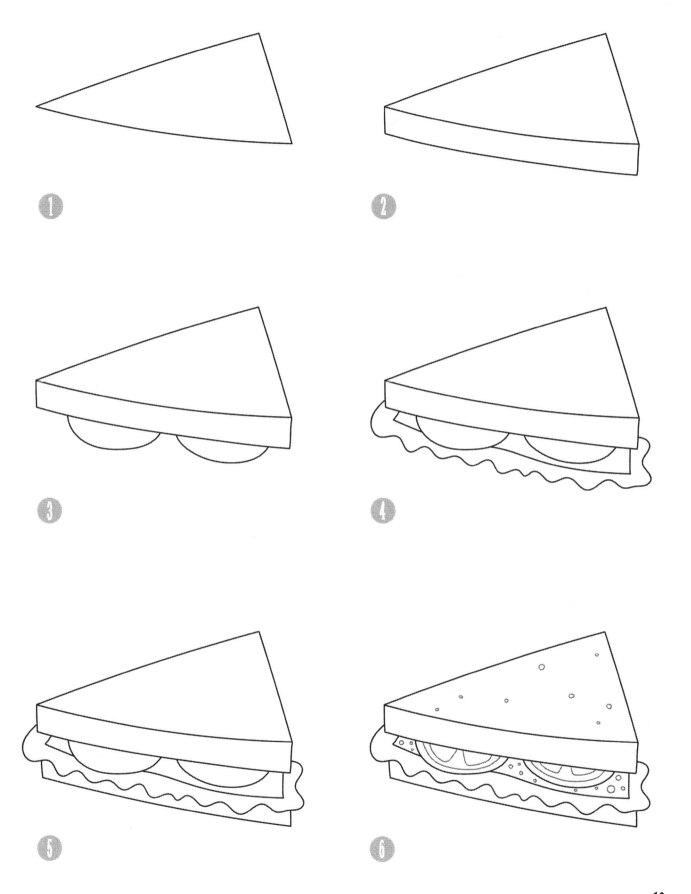

CABBAGE

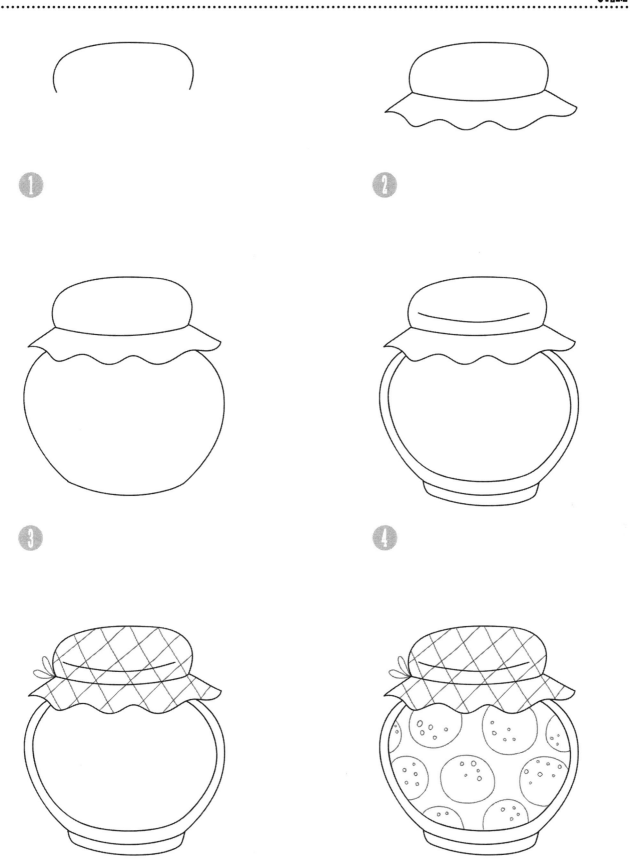

DONUT

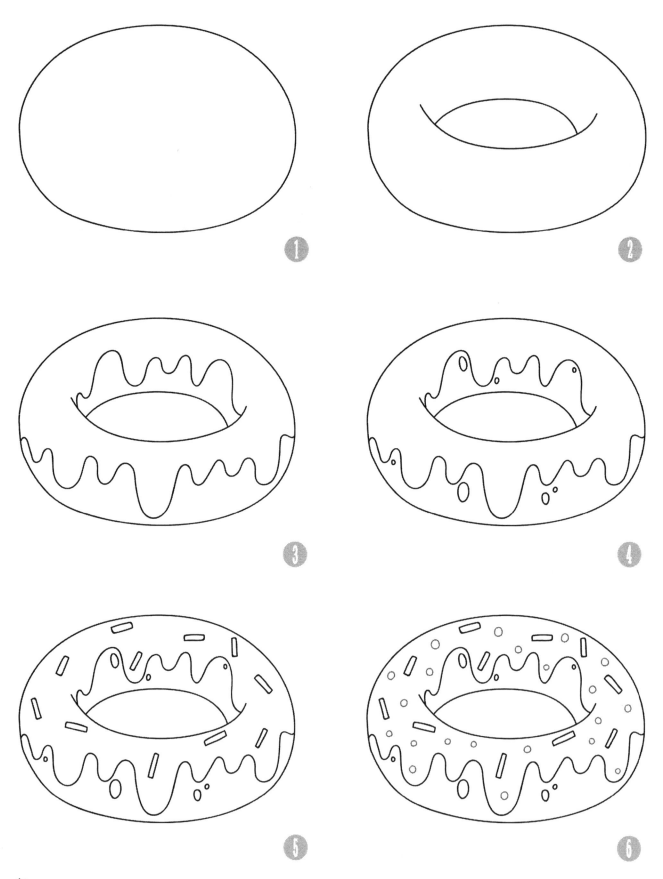

16

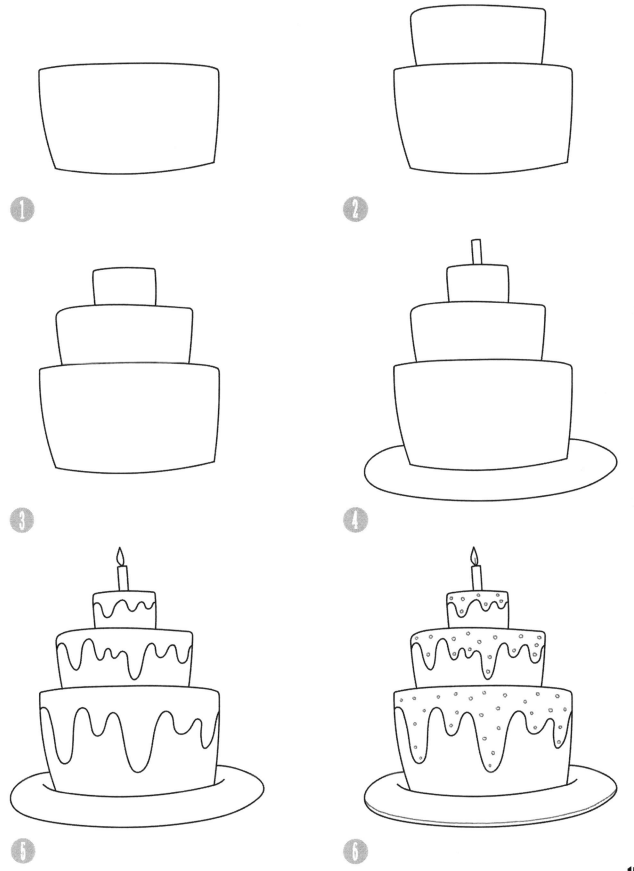

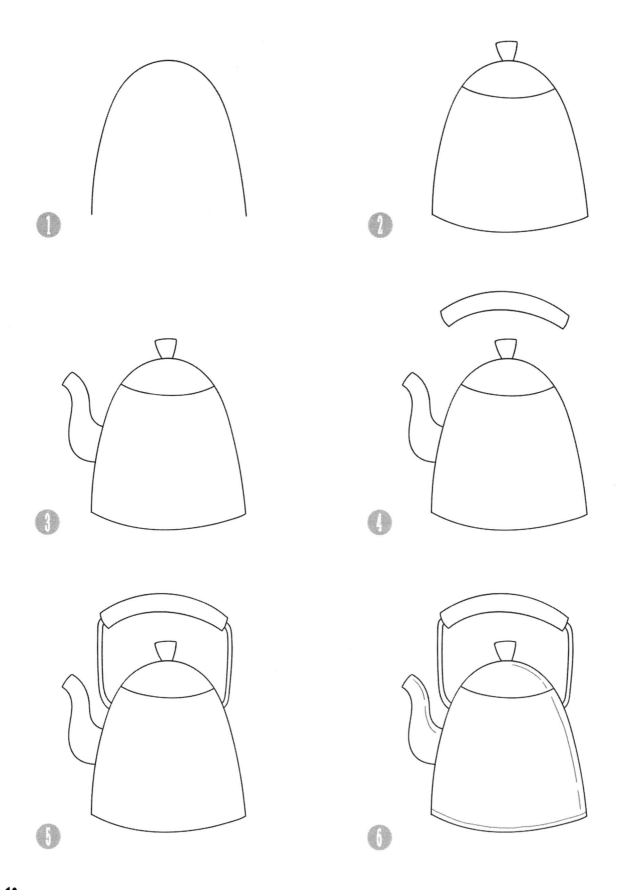

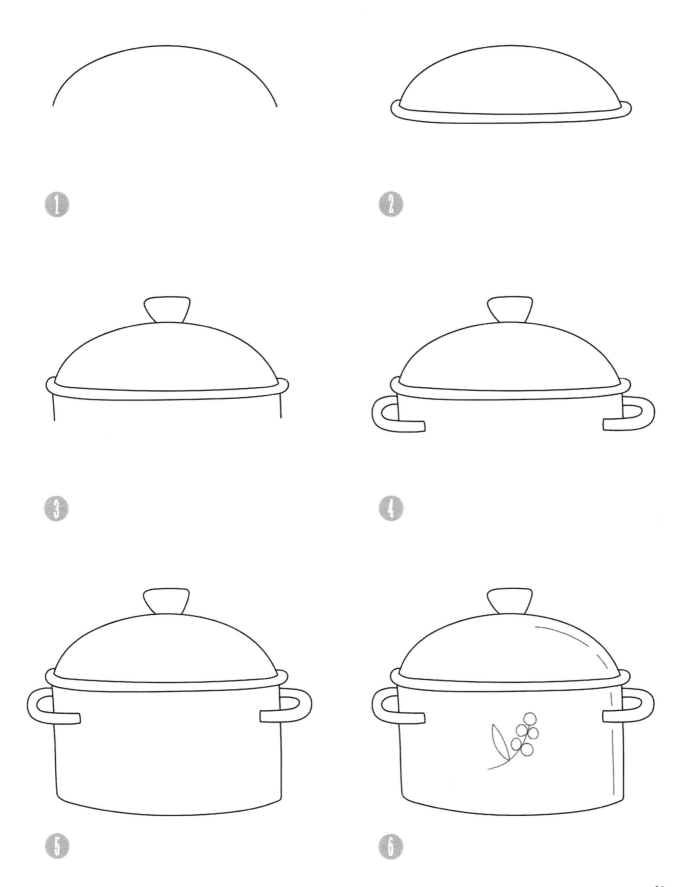

MOON

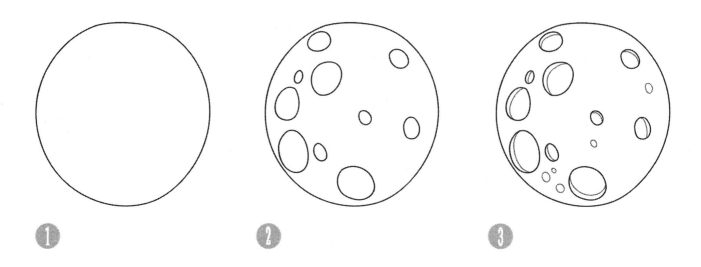

STAR

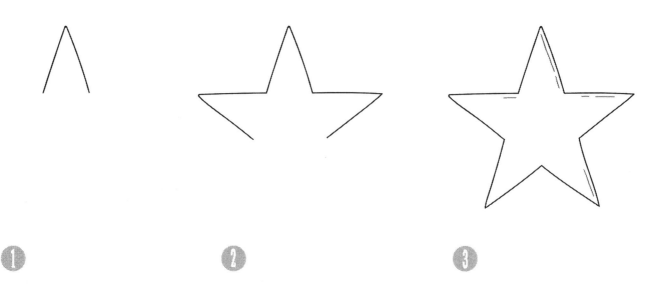

22

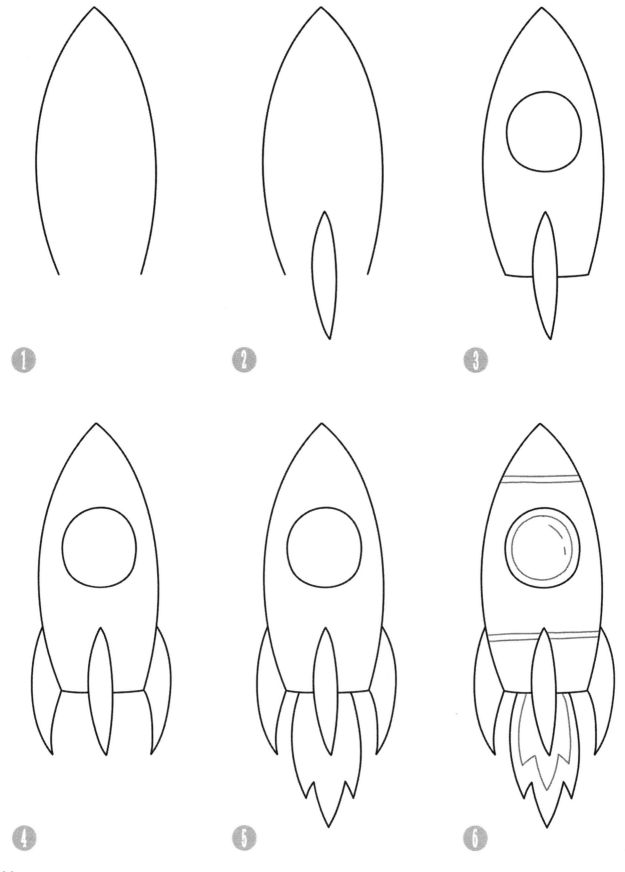

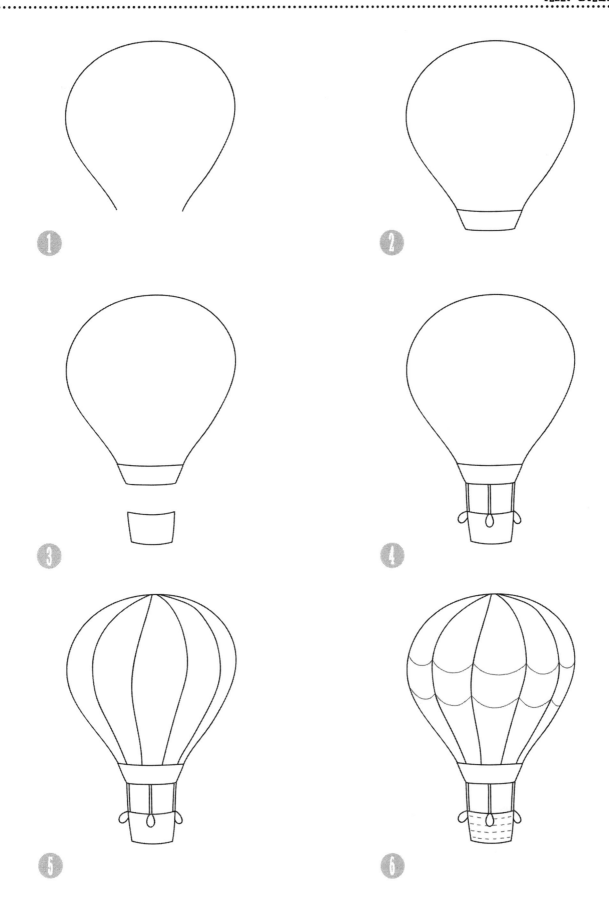

RAINBOW

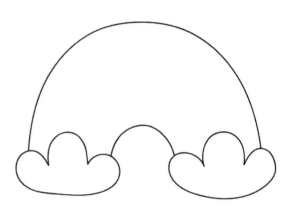

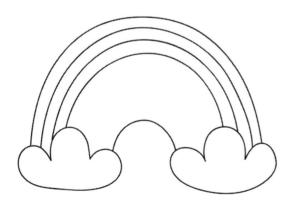

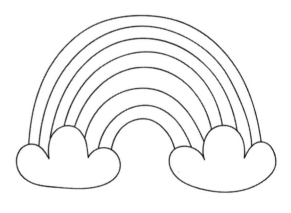

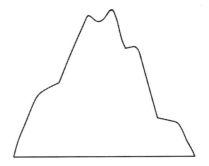

1

2

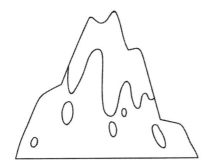

3

4

5

6

BUSH

28

①

②

③

④

⑤

⑥

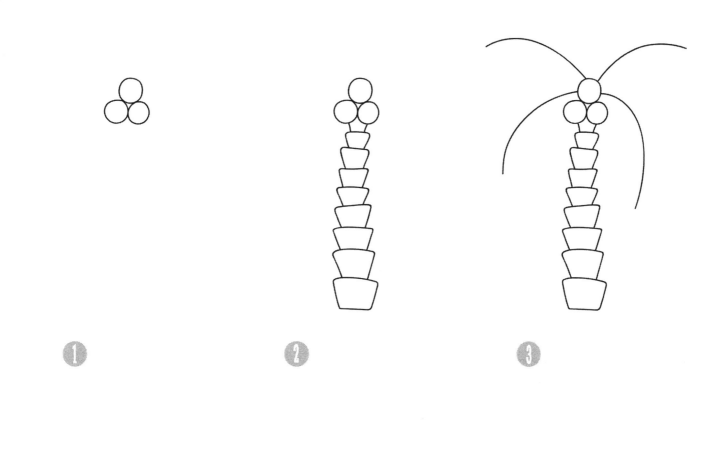

31

TULIP

33

ROSE

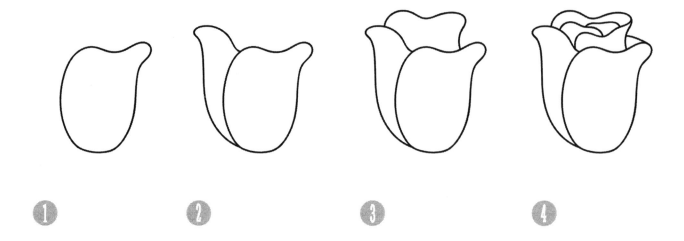

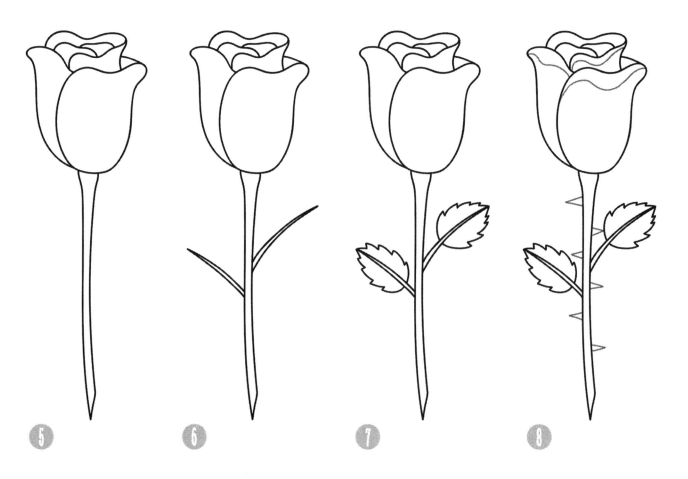

34

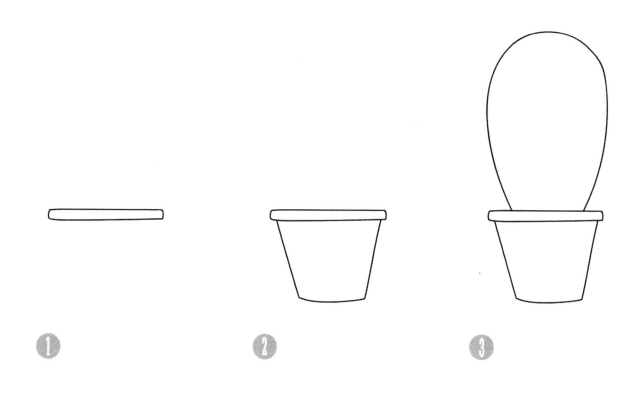

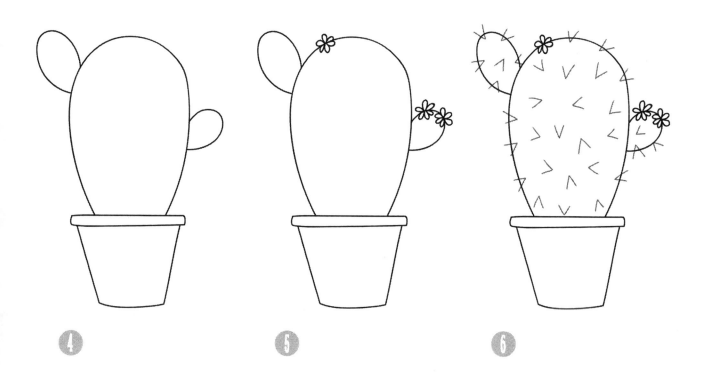

BOAT

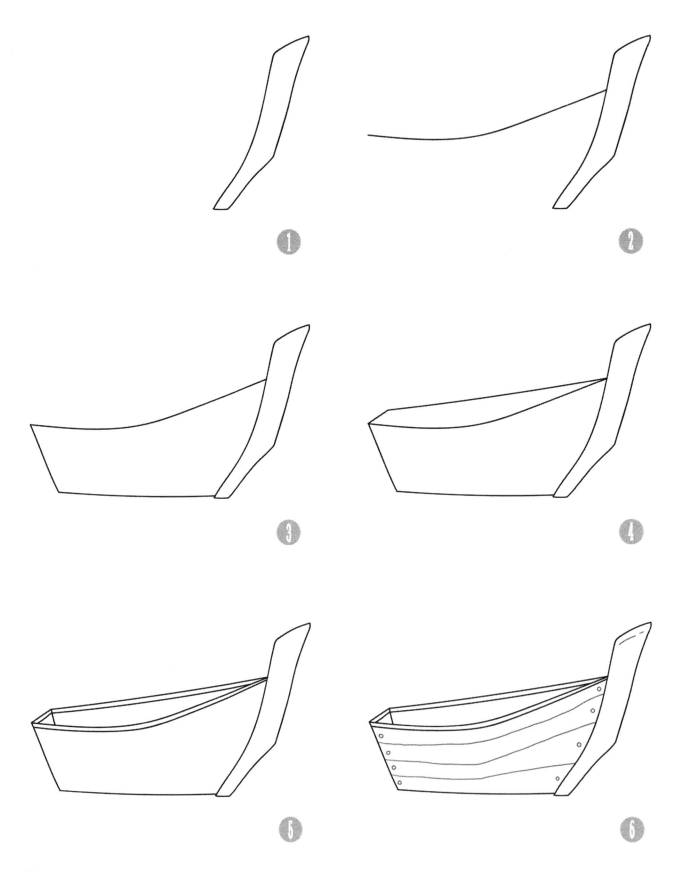

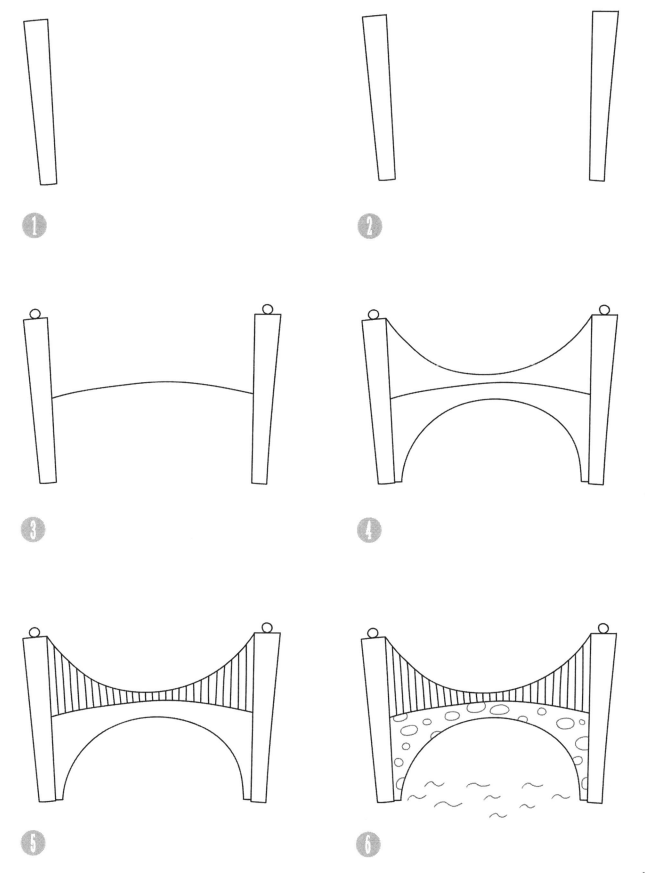

BIKE

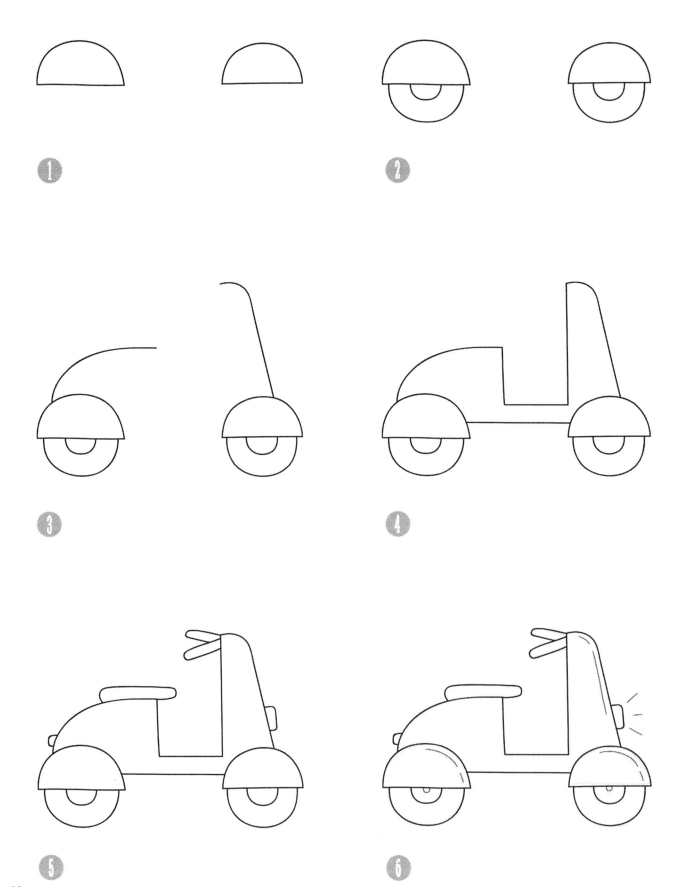

40

PLANE

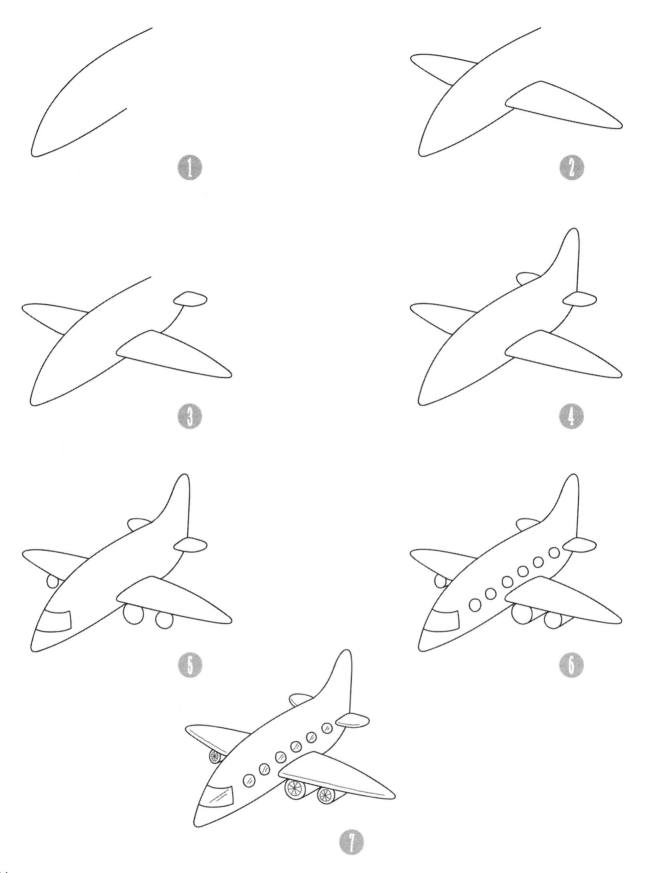

RUGBY BALL

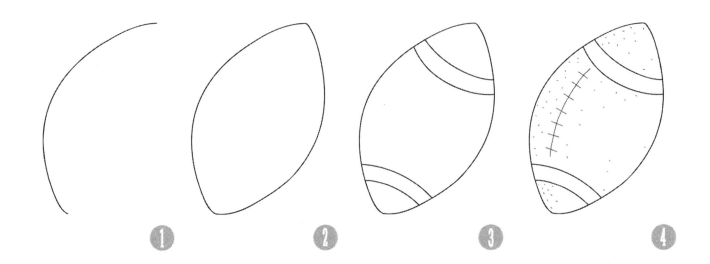

BASKETBALL BALL

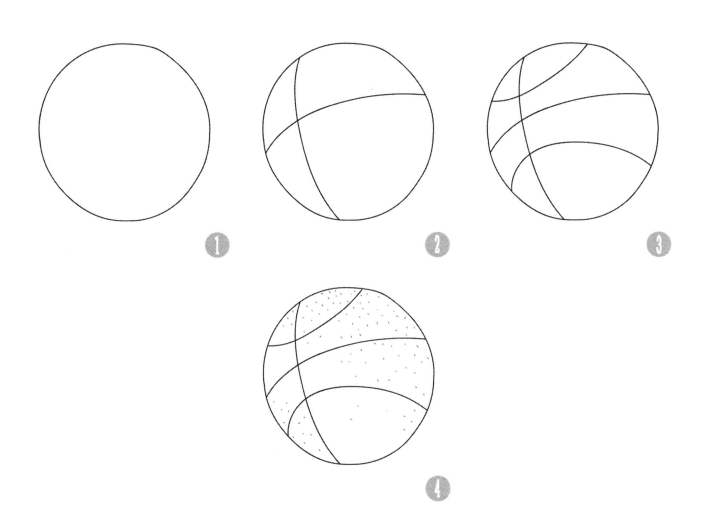

46

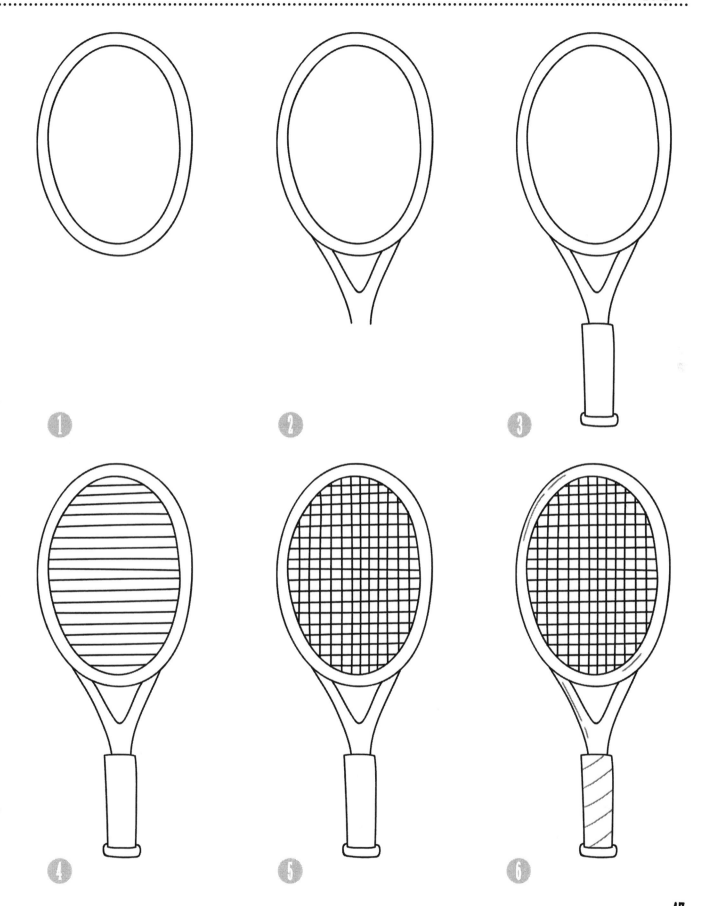

ERASER

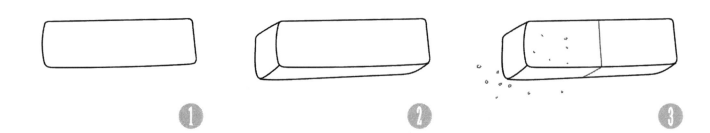

TRIANGULAR RULER

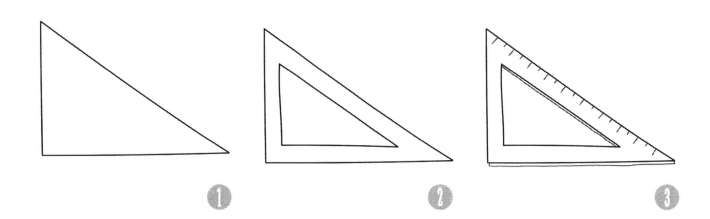

SHARPENER

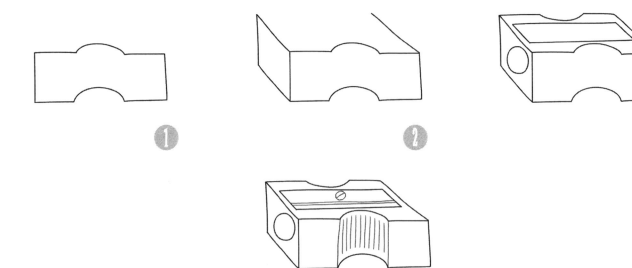

48

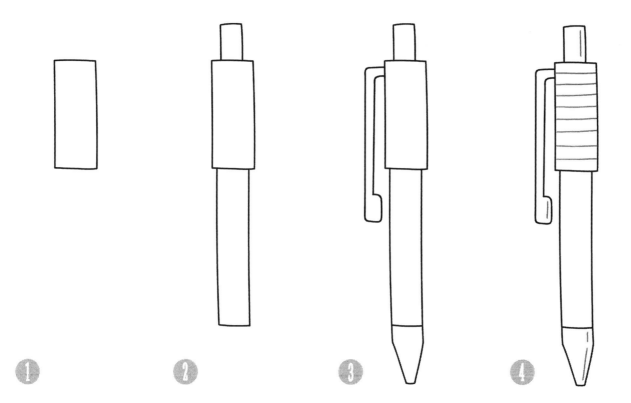

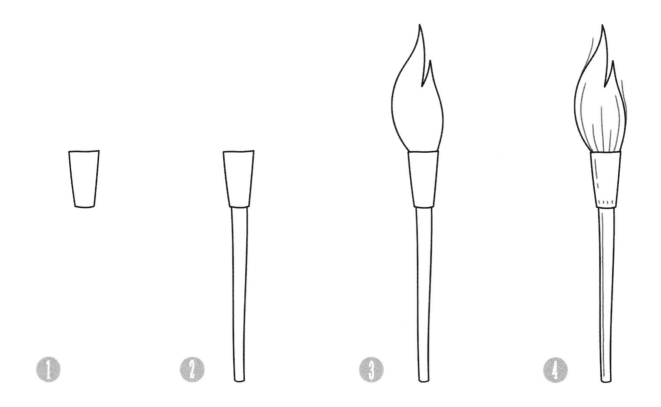

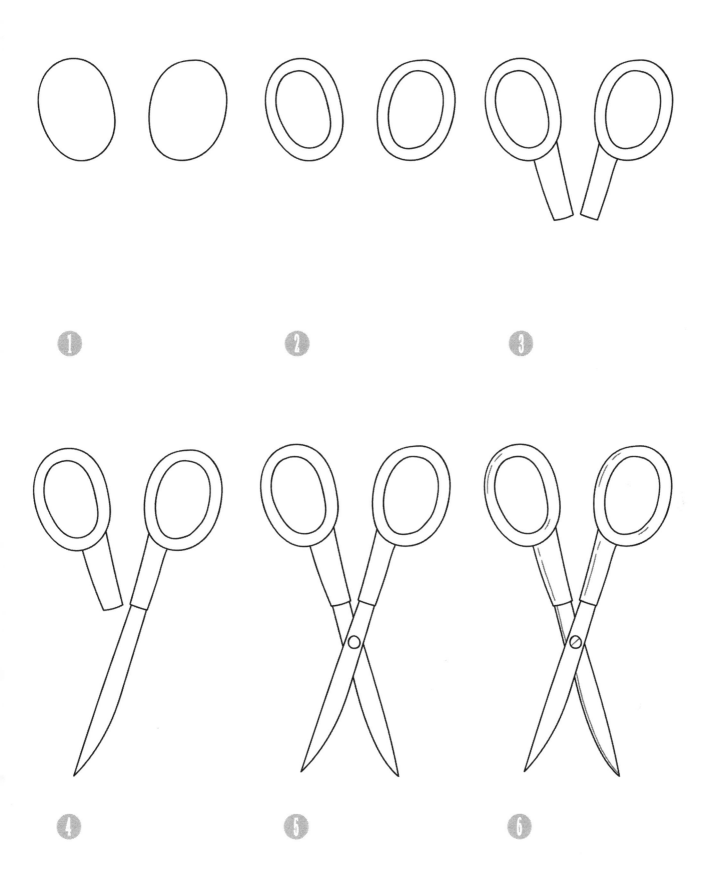

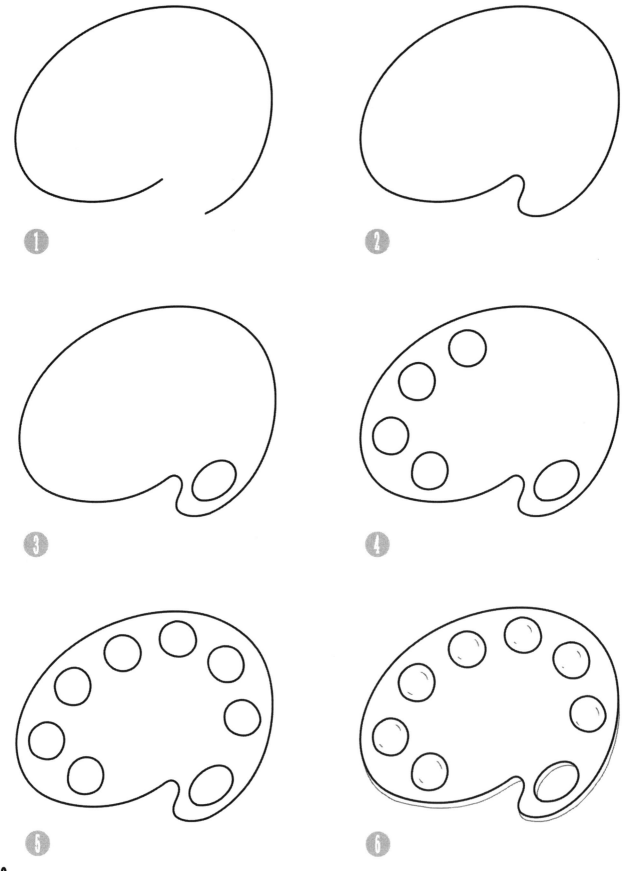

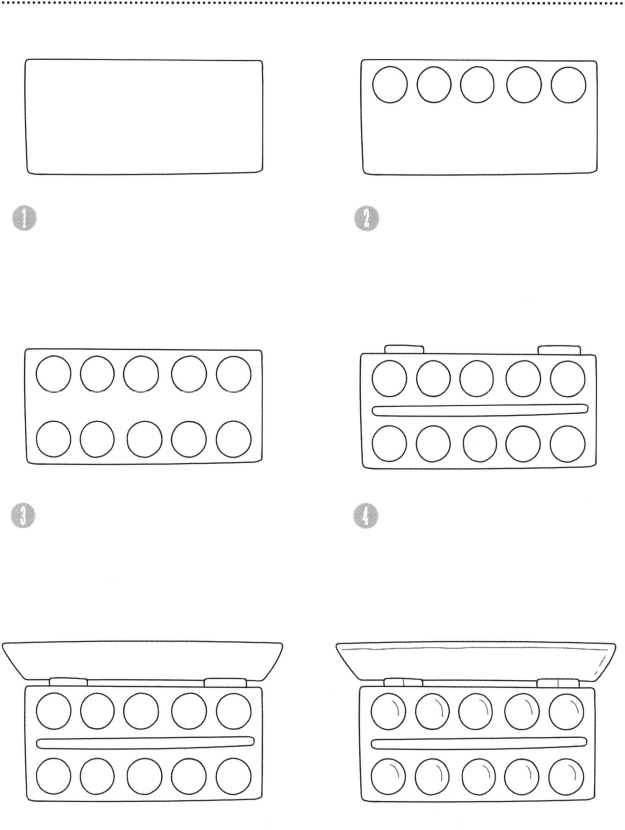

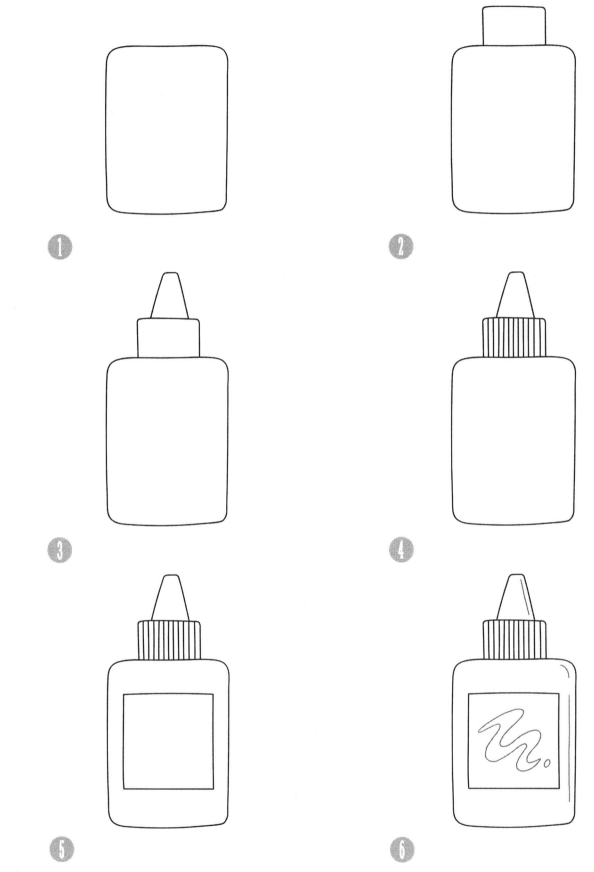

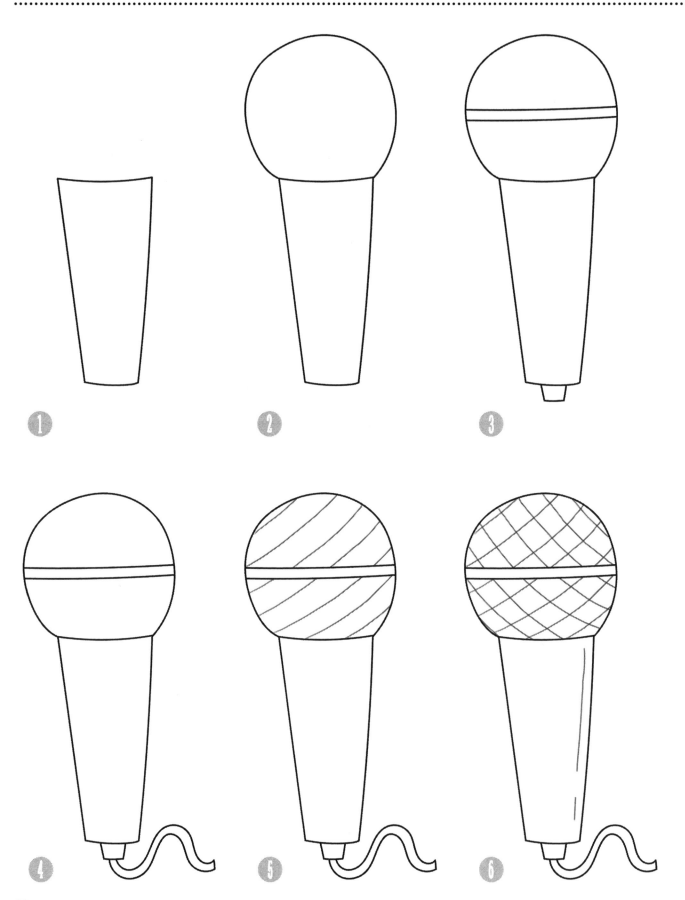

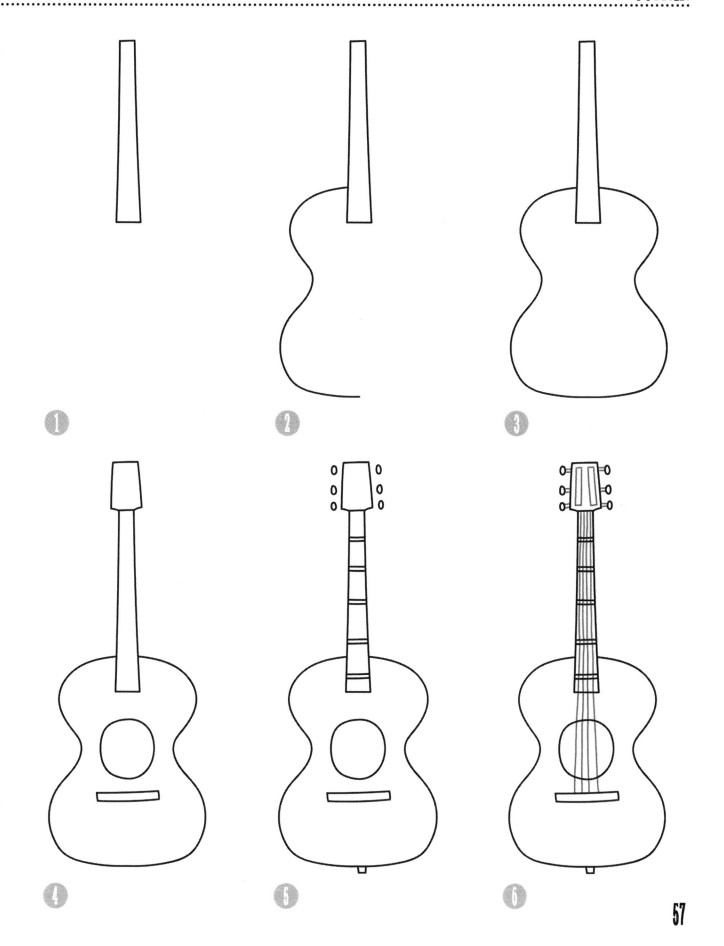

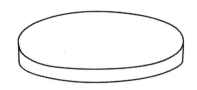

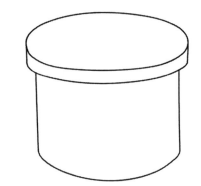

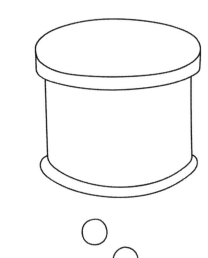

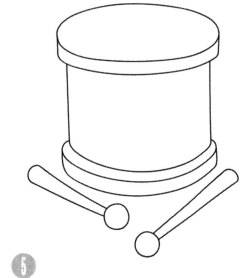

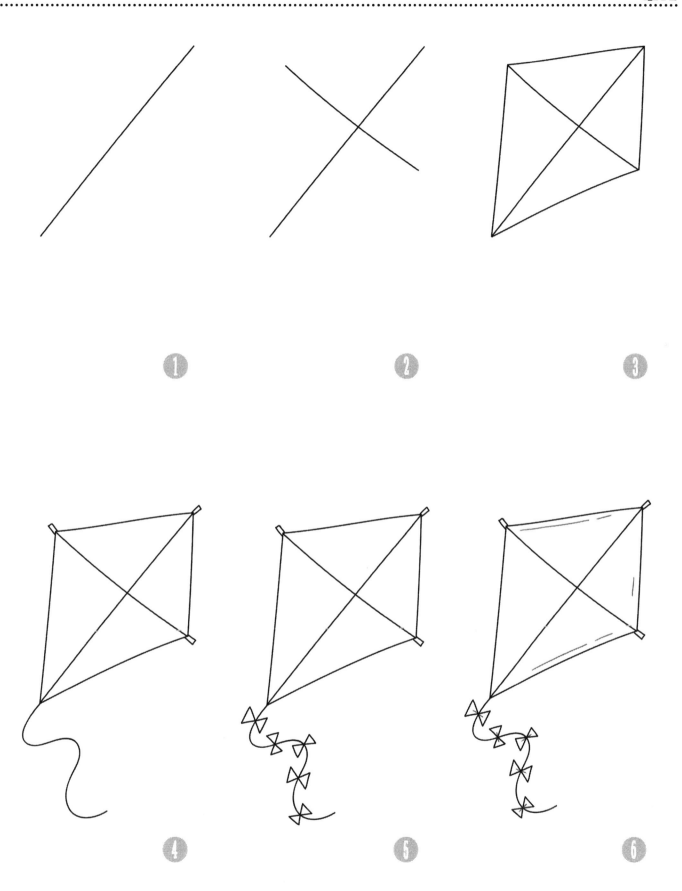

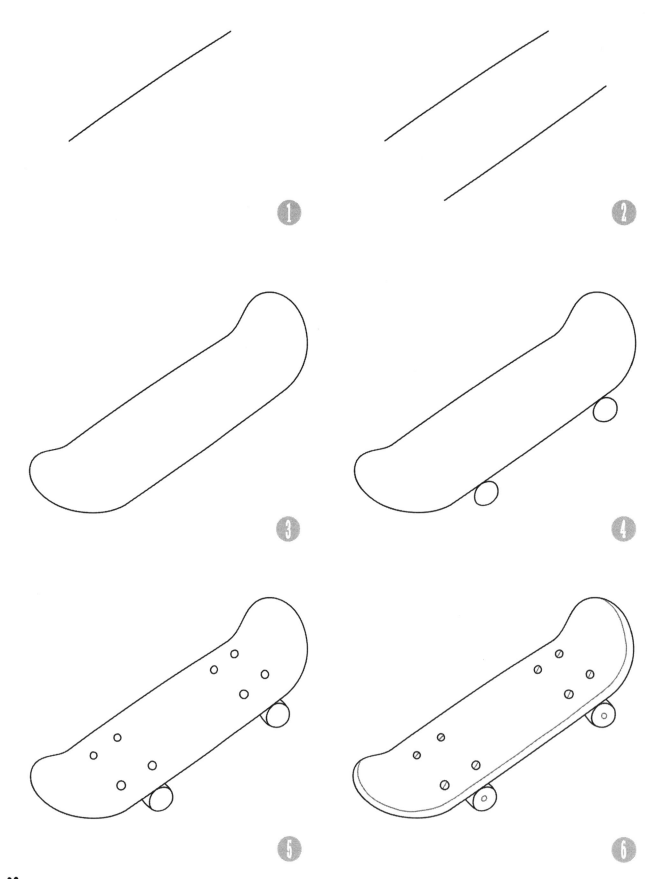

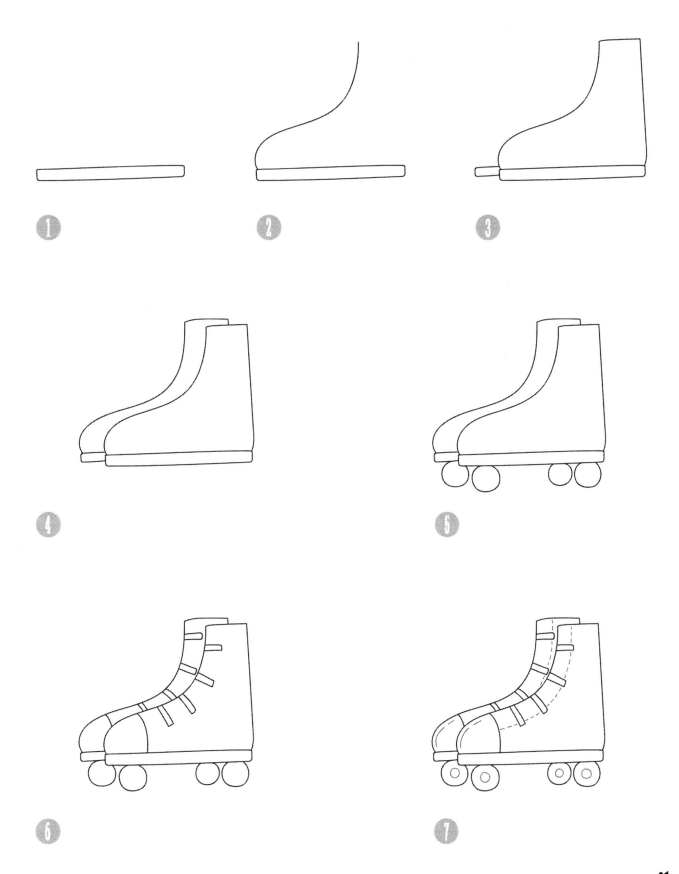

TOOChBRUSH

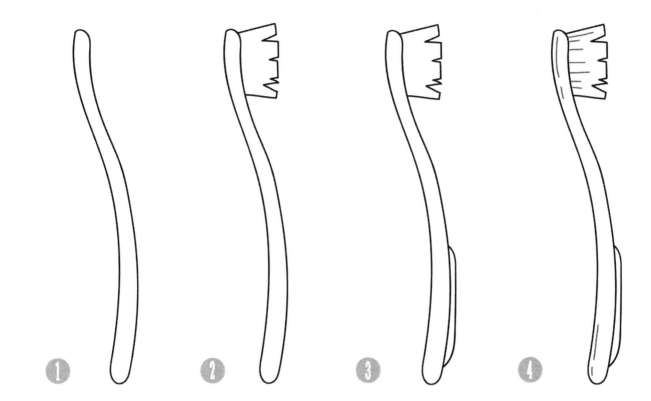

TOOTHPASTE

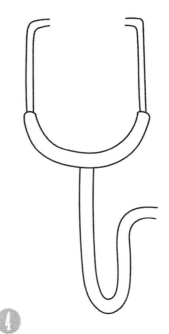

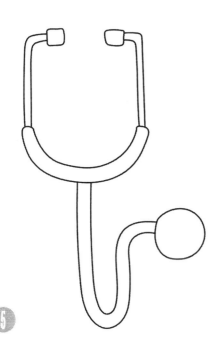

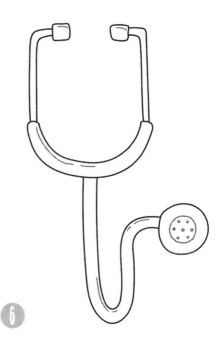

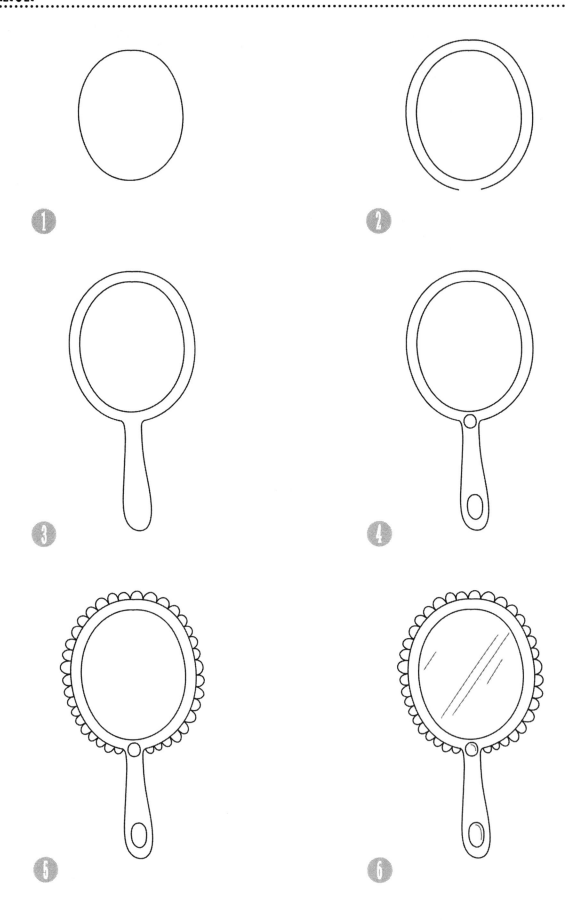

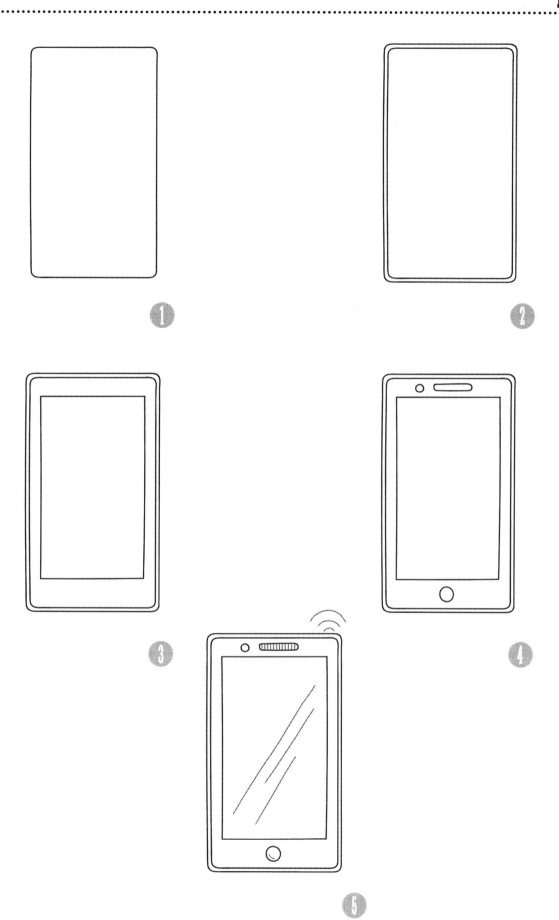

WATERING CAN

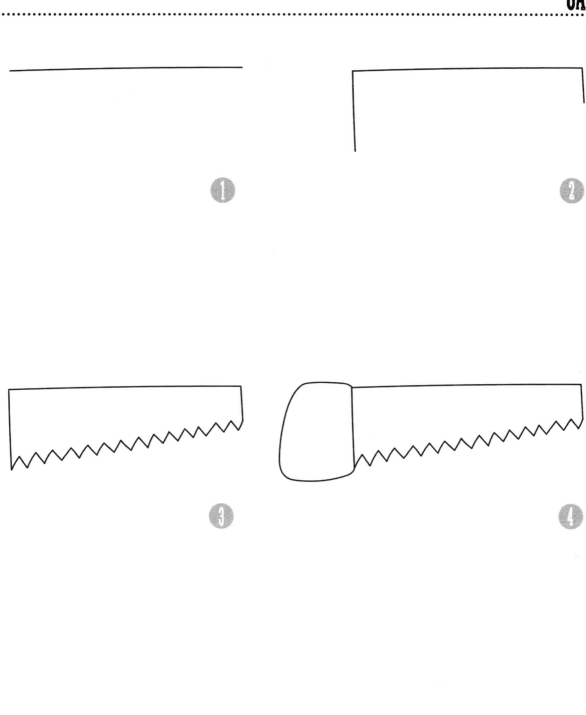

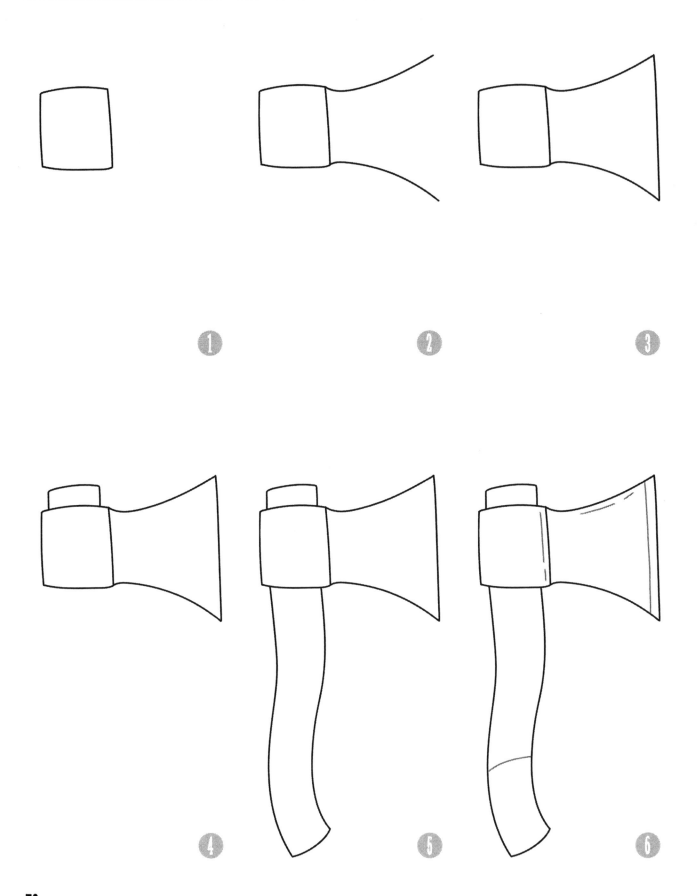

①

②

③

④

⑤

⑥

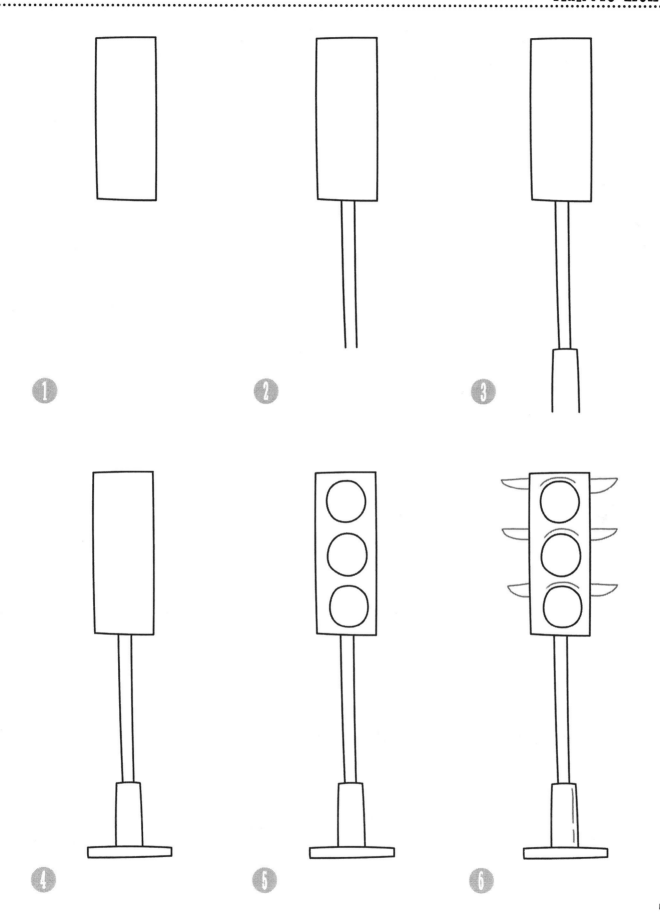

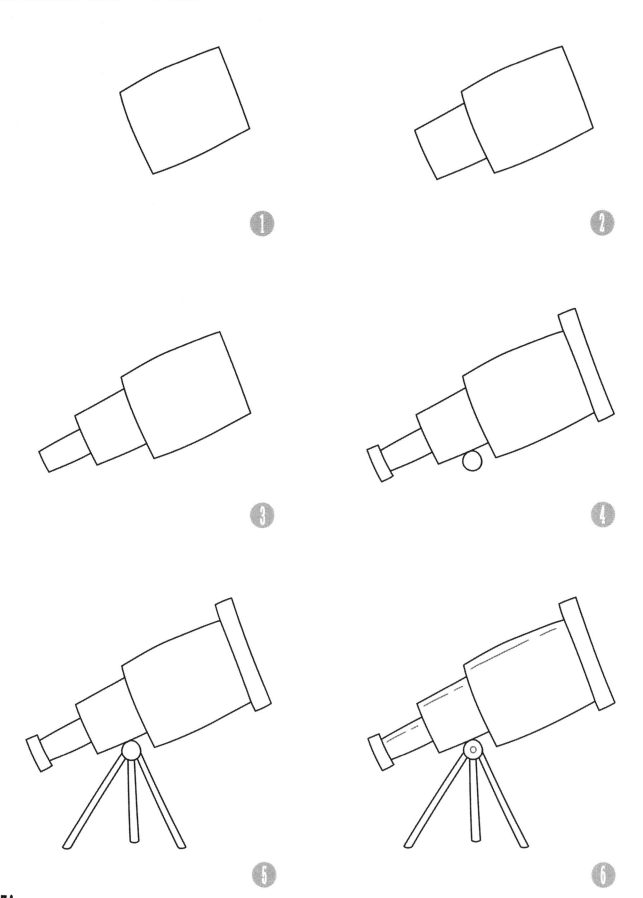

1

2

3

4

5

6

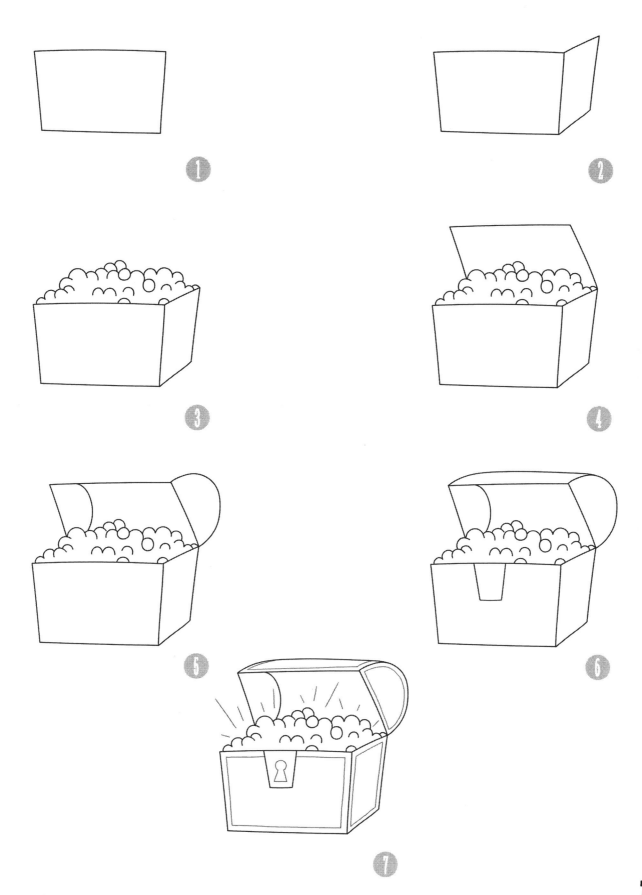

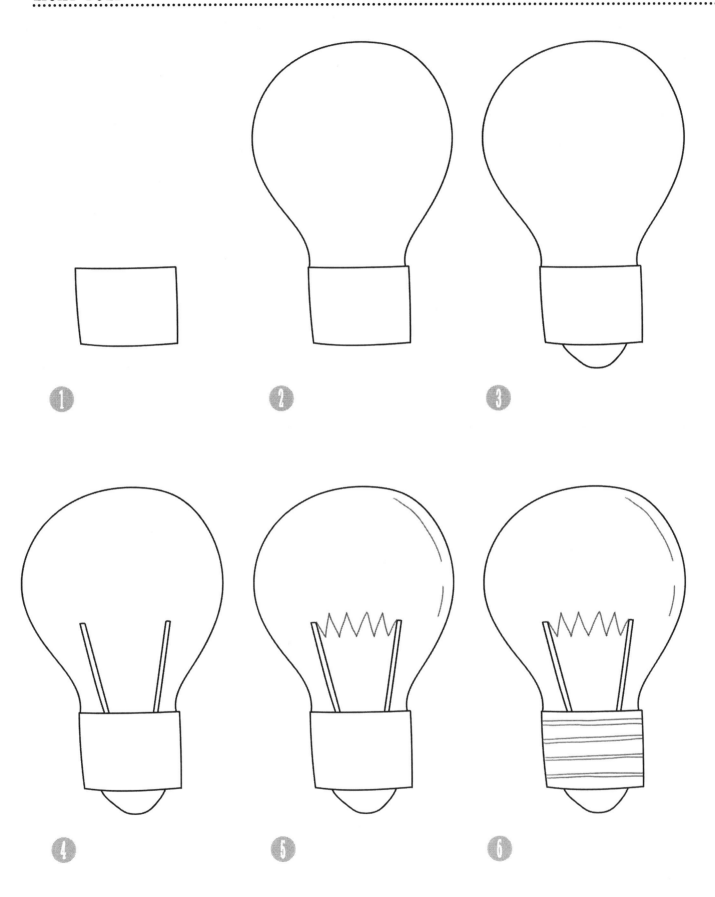

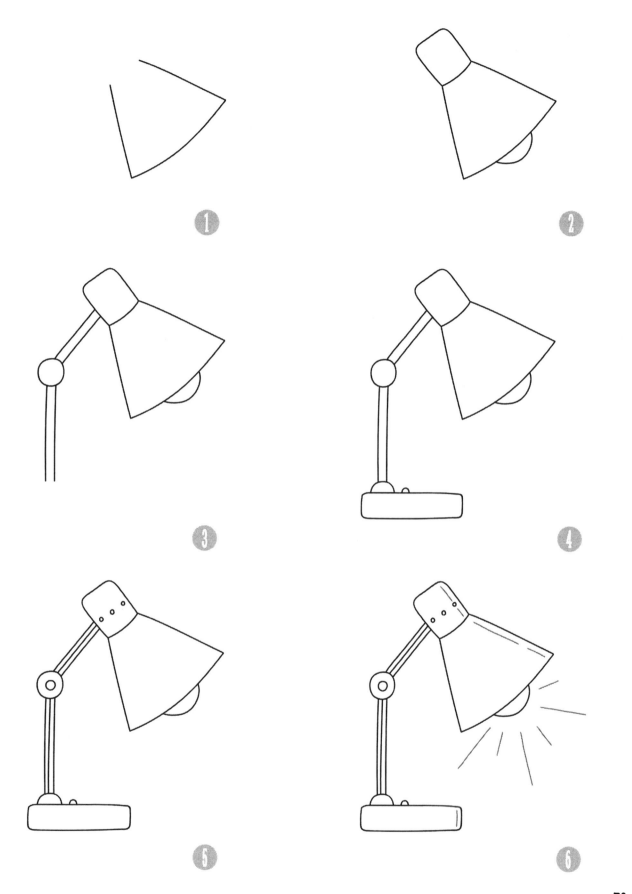

1

2

3

4

5

6

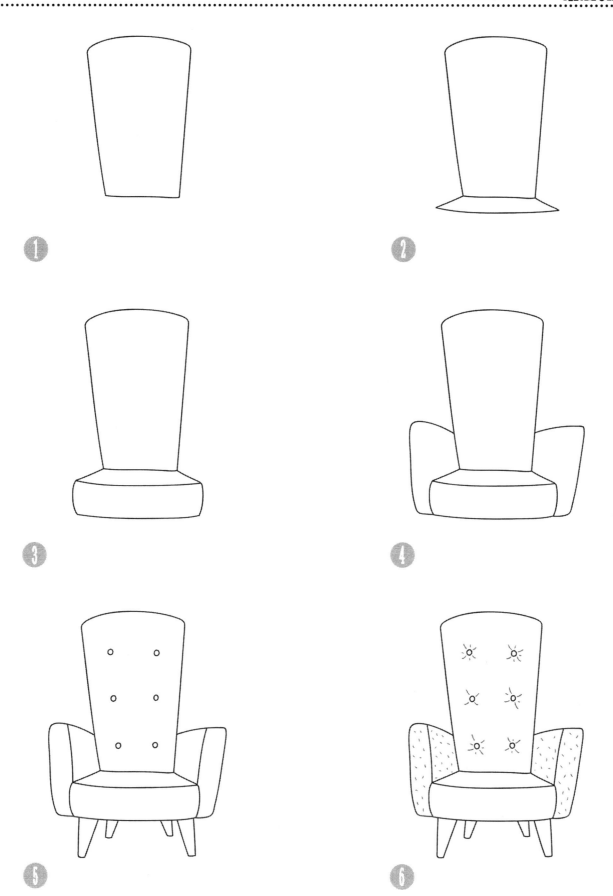

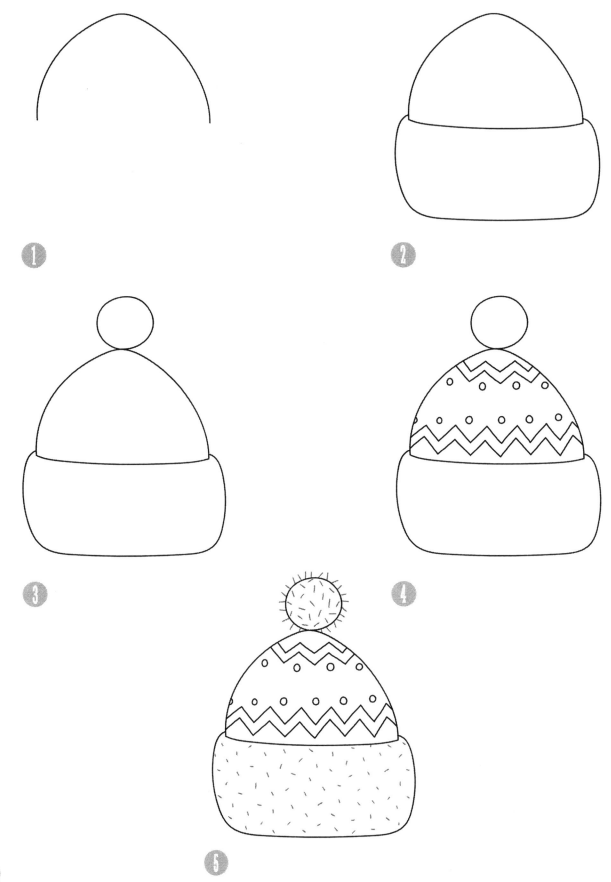

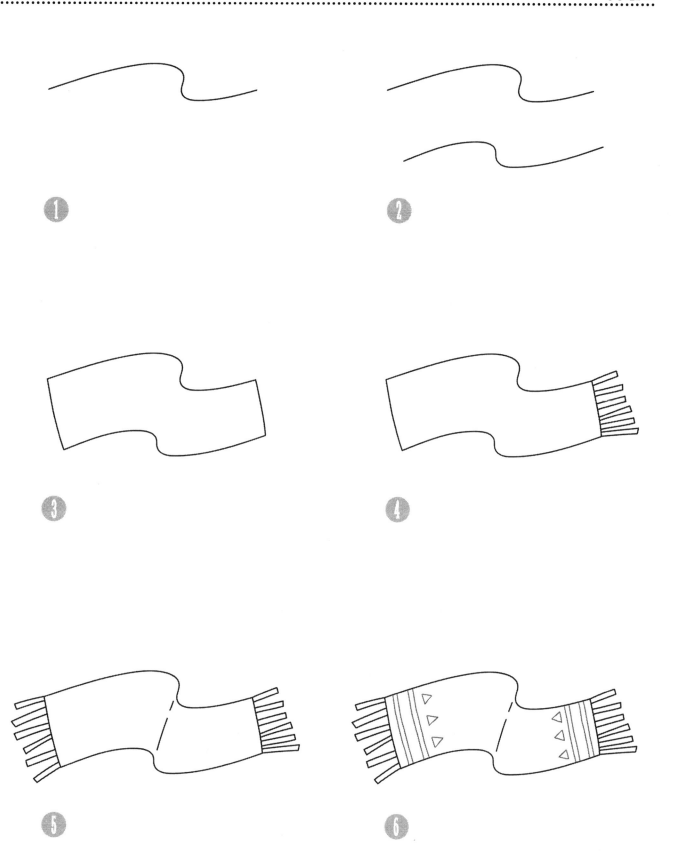

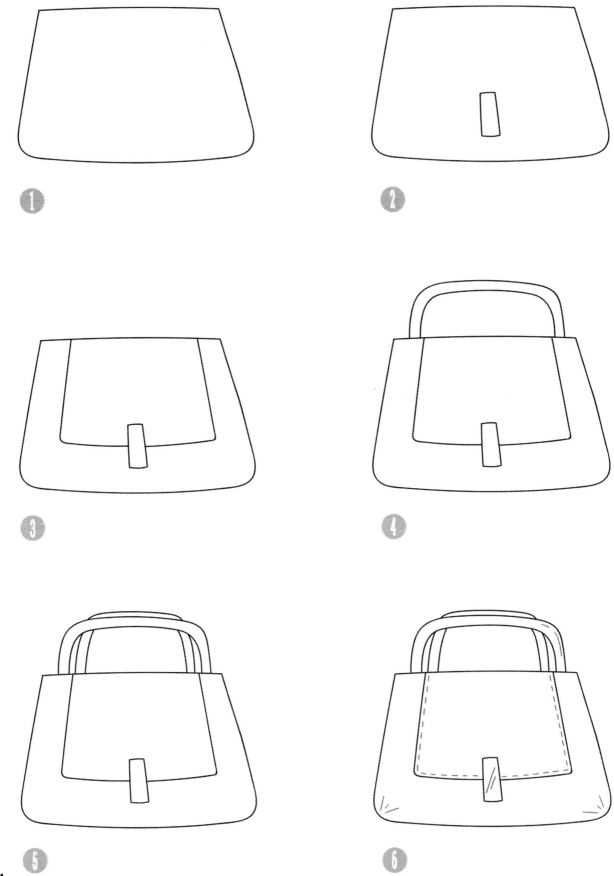

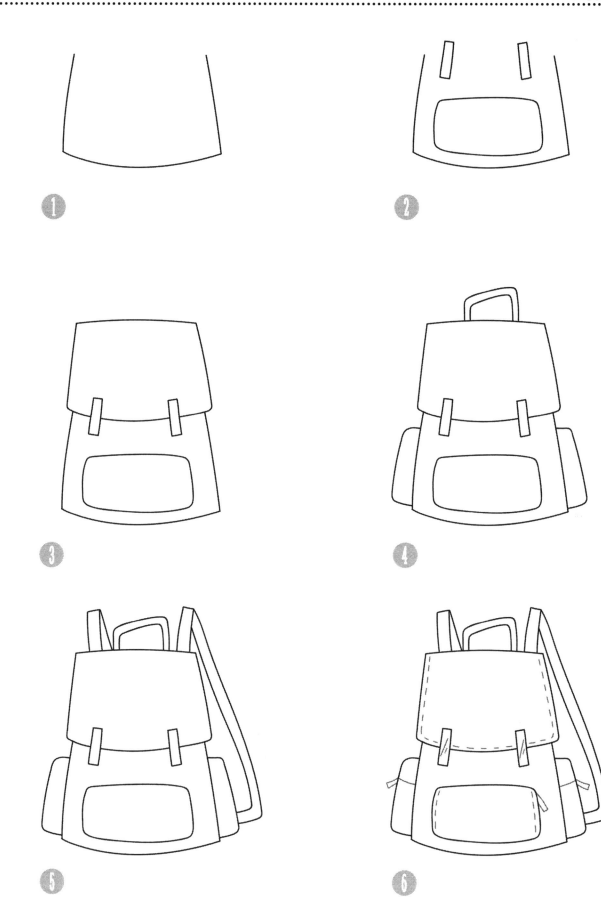

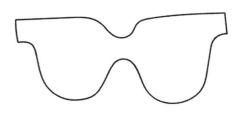

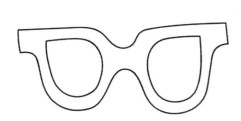

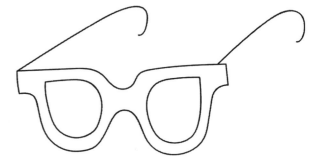

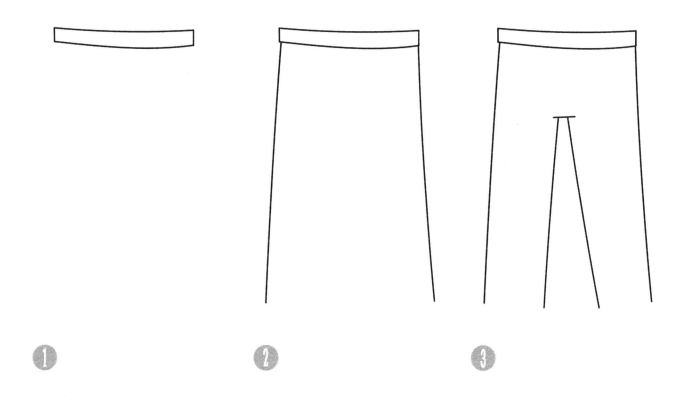

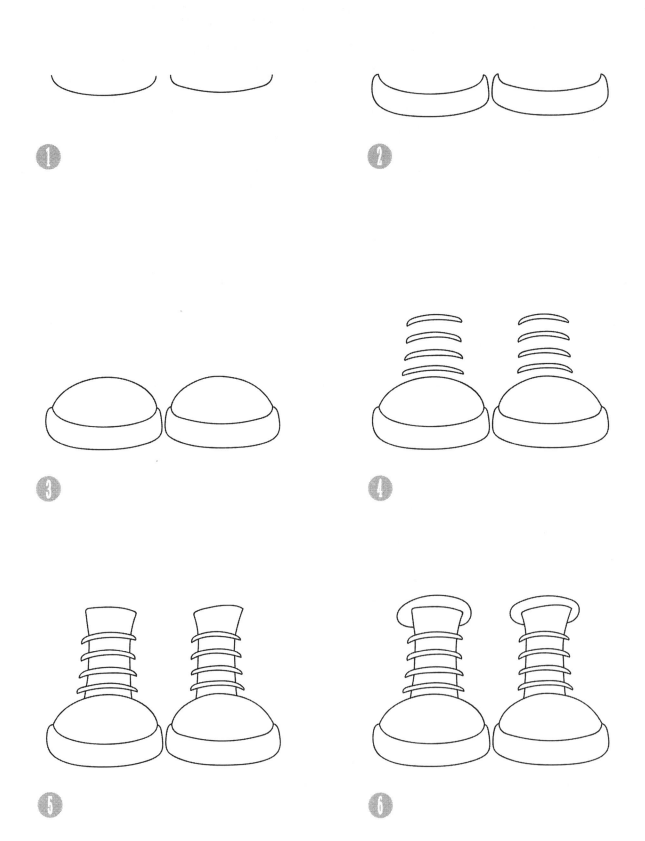

7

8

9

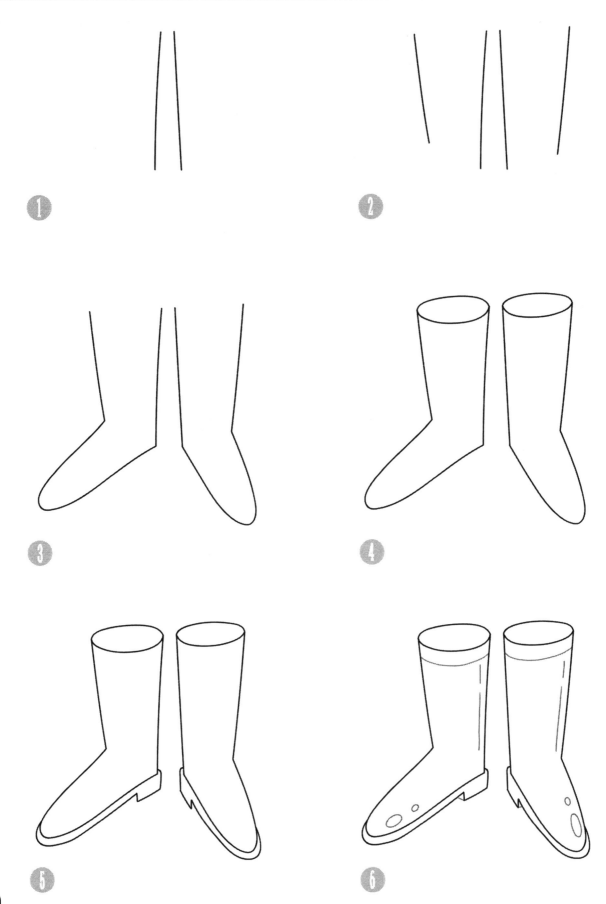

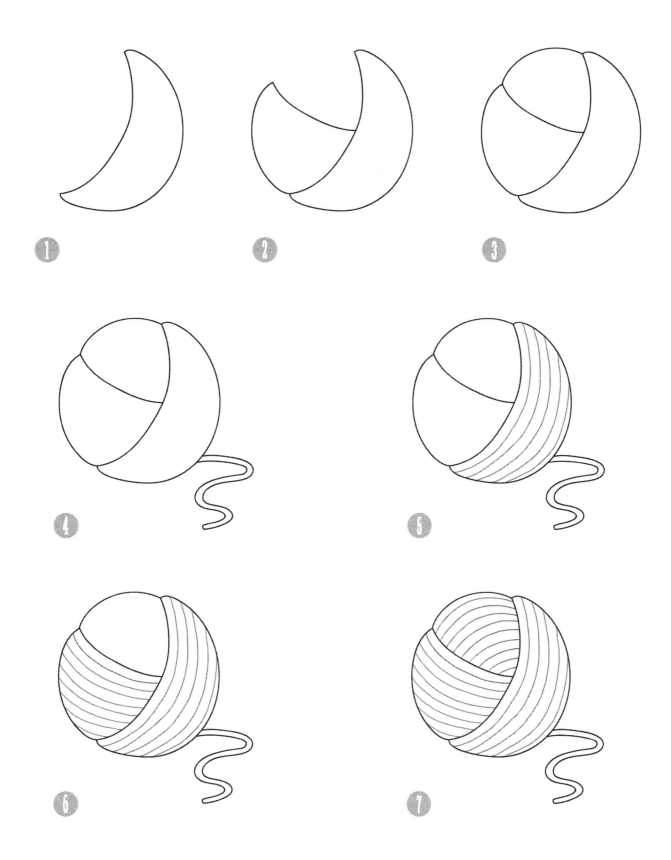

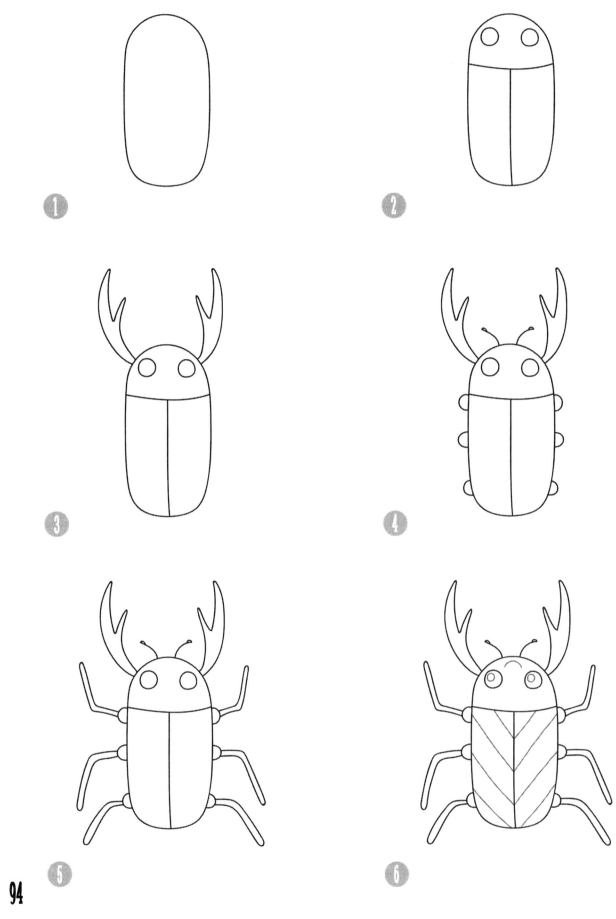

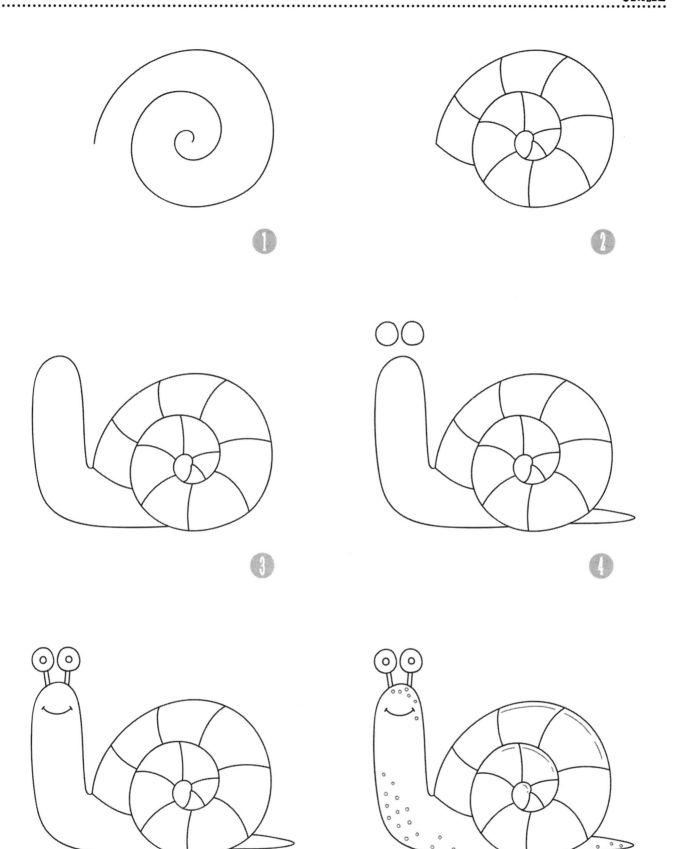

BUTTERFLY

WHALE

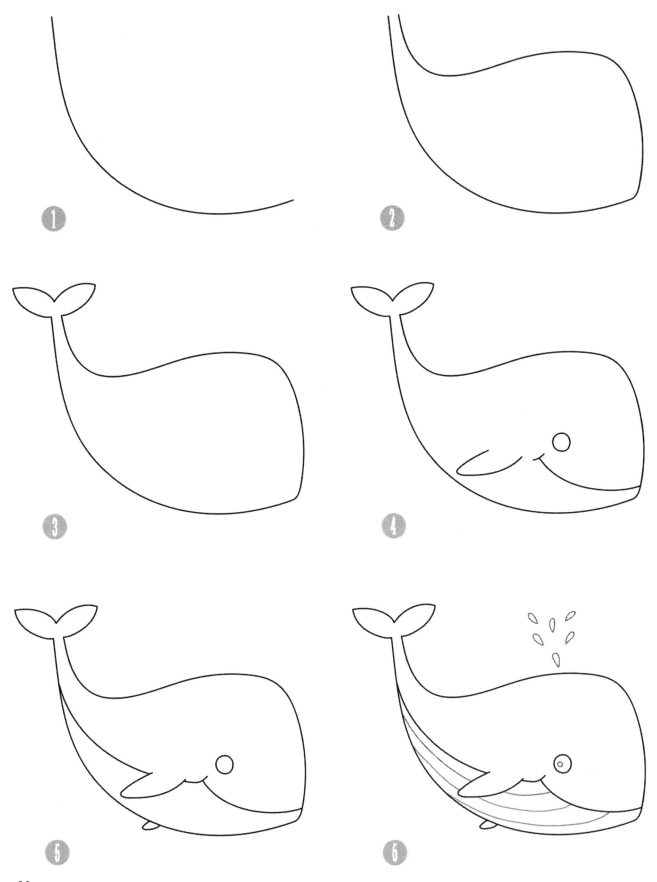

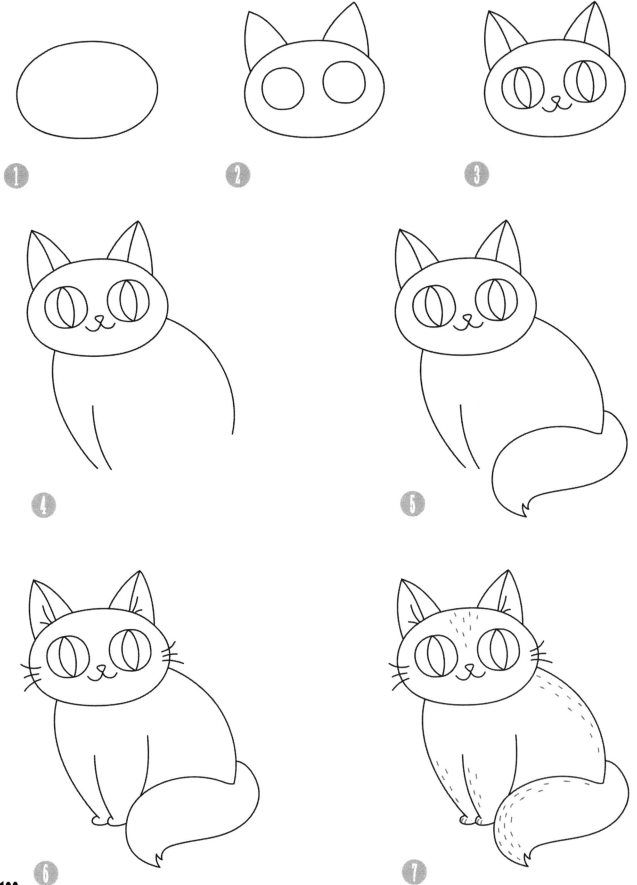

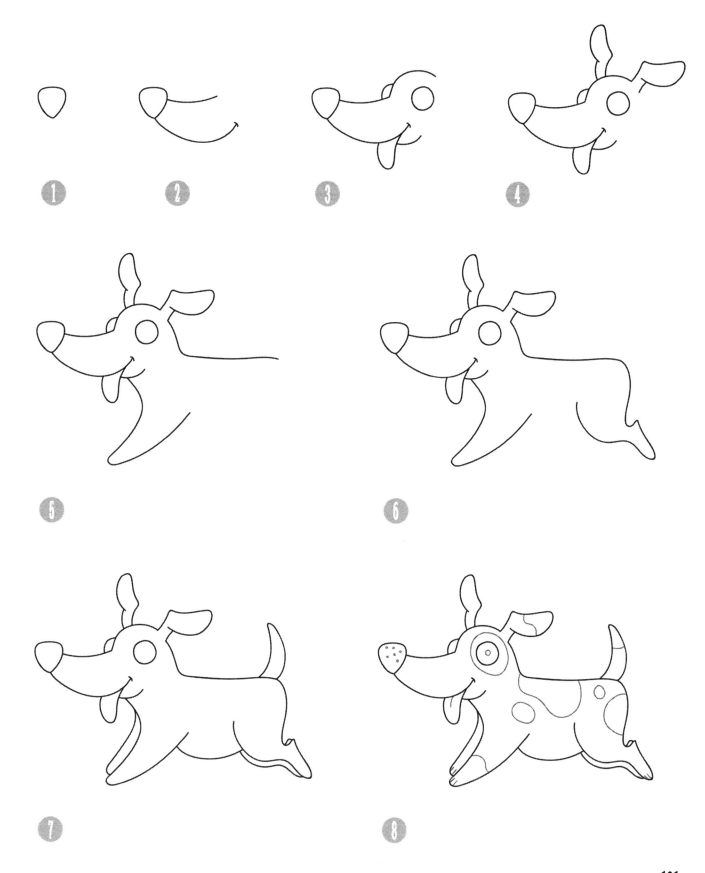

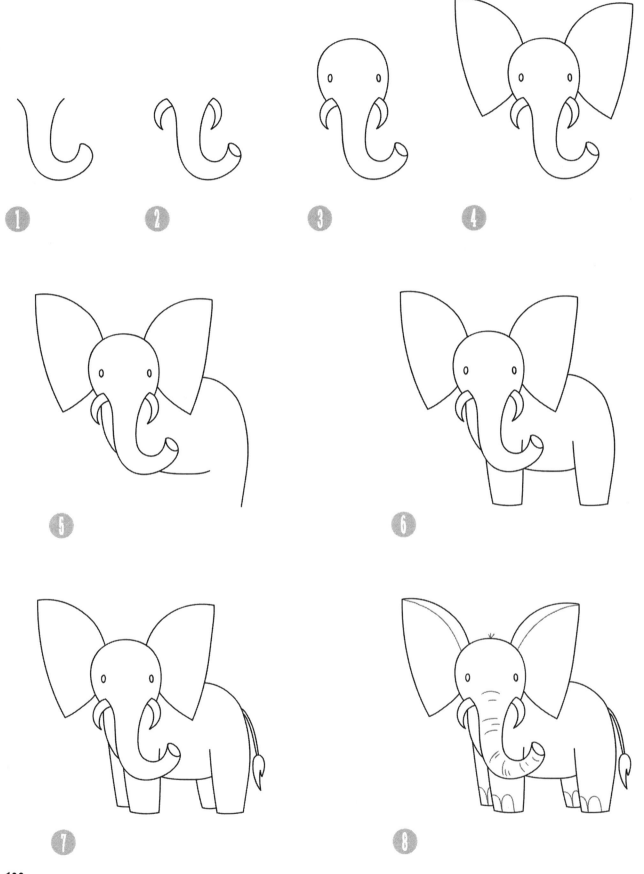

1

2

3

4

5

6

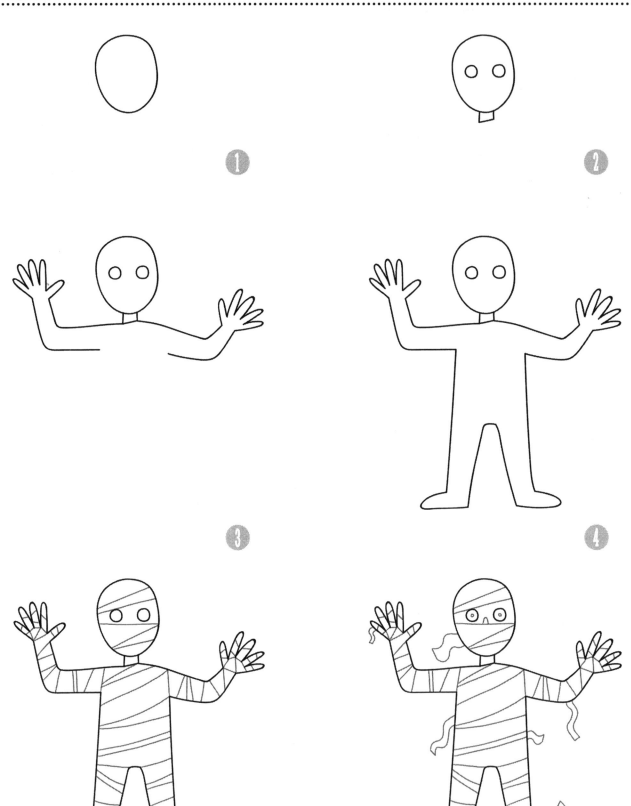

CLOWN

7

9

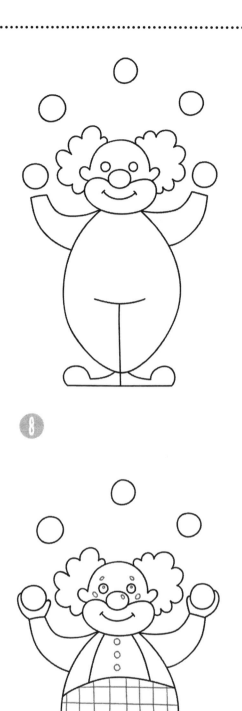

8

10

WITCH

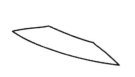

①

②

③

④

⑤

⑥

7

8

9

10

117

UNICORN

1

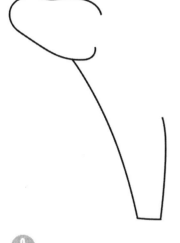

2

3

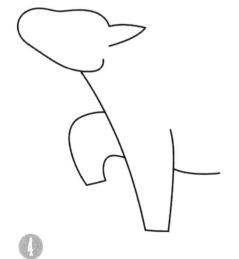

4

5

DRAGON

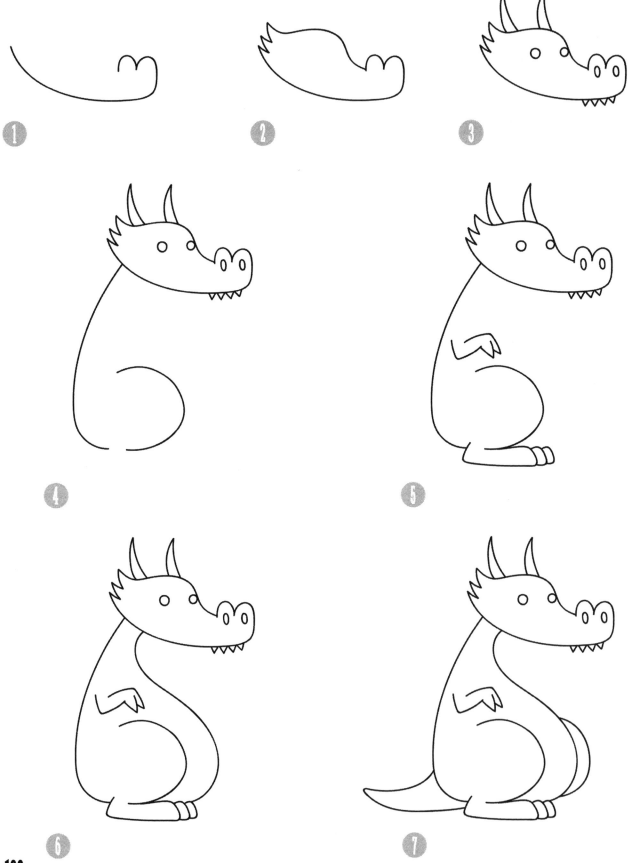

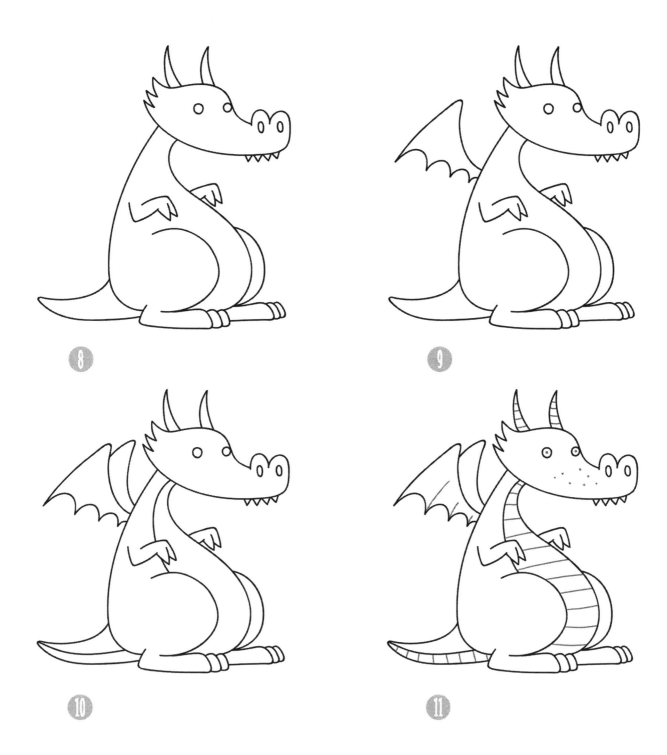

WRITTEN AND ILLUSTRATED
BY
VERA SYSOLINA

Made in United States
Orlando, FL
08 January 2024

42273329R00067